The Story of

IN GOD WE TRUST

JOHN HUDSON TINER

First Printing: March 2003
Second Printing: November 2006

Cover and Interior design by Bryan Miller
Photo credits: Library of Congress: p.11,
National Park Service p. 27
ISBN 13: 978-0-89051-392-7
ISBN 10: 0-89051-392-9
Library of Congress Number: 2002116469

Printed in China
Please visit our website for other great titles
www.newleafpress.net

Master
Books

Table of Contents

The Story Of In God We Trust

The United States has a strong **economy**, and its money is accepted everywhere around the world. About two-thirds of United States currency circulates in foreign countries. In nations where the government is weak, United States **currency** is favored over local money. More United States paper money is used in other countries than inside the United States itself.

Much can be learned about a country by the words and pictures found on its money. United States bills and coins bear the statement "In God We Trust." The inspiring words are carried into some countries where Christian missionaries are not allowed. How the phrase became the national motto is a story that spans 200 years.

On American Paper Money

The phrase "In God We Trust" has not always been on paper money. Until the 1950s, it was found only on coins. The end of World War II (1939–1945) marked the start of the dark days of the Cold War. During this time, **communist** countries rigidly controlled their citizens. Dictators tried to destroy any references to God. Religious freedom in Russia, China, North Korea, and other countries ceased to exist. Communist leaders built walls topped by barbed wire to prevent their people from escaping to the free world.

People with vision looked for ways to give Christian believers in communist countries a reason for hope. Matthew H. Rothert was a friendly man who ran a furniture store in Camden, Arkansas. In 1953, he and his wife visited her family in Chicago, Illinois. At a Sunday morning church service, Rothert noticed that "In God We Trust" was on coins. But paper money did not carry the motto.

Matthew Rothert knew that United States currency circulated all over the globe. A message on paper money about this country's faith in God could easily be carried to everyone. He wrote to George C. Humphrey, Secretary of the Treasury, about the idea. Secretary Humphrey liked Rothert's suggestion. But he explained, "To put the motto on a bill would require an Act of **Congress**."

The idea seemed headed for an unhappy ending. However, Rothert became seriously sick. He put his trust in God to carry him through the difficult times. He was not idle while he recovered in bed from his illness. He wrote letters to senators, representatives, and newspapers. He said,

"Why shouldn't paper money bear the same inscription as coins? Our paper money should carry a spiritual message to all nations."

He wrote to President Dwight D. Eisenhower. Rothert said, "Most people believe that the motto 'In God We Trust' is on both our coins and our paper money. However, this is not the case, and I believe the addition of this motto in the proper place on our paper money at this time would be a forward step in our international relations."

J. William Fulbright, one of the senators who represented Matthew Rothert's home state of Arkansas, was all for the idea. He said, "I think your idea is a very good one." Senator Fulbright introduced a bill authorizing the use of the motto on paper money. Congress voted its approval, and President Eisenhower signed the bill into law on July 30, 1956.

In 1957, "In God We Trust" appeared first on the back of a one-dollar bill. By 1963, all other **denominations** carried the motto. Today, all coins and currency show the

belief in God that is deeply rooted in the history of the United States.

Money Overseas. Of the 540 billion dollars in total United States currency, about 360 billion is held in foreign countries. Most of that is in denominations of one-hundred dollar bills.

Paper Money. The United States prints about 37  million bills each day with a value of about 696 million dollars. About half of the bills are one-dollar bills. Most are printed to replace old, worn out bills. Paper money is sometimes called "folding money" because it is folded when a billfold is closed. A bill can be folded about 4,000 times before it wears out. Most one-dollar bills are worn out within two years. Larger denominations last longer. The 100 dollar bill has a lifetime of nine years.

The Iron Curtain. Winston Churchill, the prime minister of England during World War II, visited the United

States in 1946. He gave a speech in Fulton, Missouri. He said, "From Stettin in the Baltic to Trieste in the Adriatic, an iron curtain has descended across the continent." The Iron Curtain became a symbolic name for the separation between the communist countries and the free world.

I like Ike! Dwight David Eisenhower was a hero of World War II. He led all the forces that successfully defeated Hitler and his armies. Eisenhower's parents taught him as a child to pray and read the Bible every day. As a youngster, he had difficulty controlling his temper. Once he became so angry that he beat his fists against a tree until they began to bleed. His mother bandaged his hands. She told him, "He that conquereth his own soul is greater than he who taketh a city." This idea is found in the Bible in Proverbs 16:32. Eisenhower later said this was the most valuable advice he had ever received.

In 1953, Eisenhower became the 34th president of the United States. People who elected him president used the slogan "I like Ike!"

On American Coins

Coins have not always carried the words "In God We Trust." The motto first appeared on coins **minted** during the dark days of the Civil War (1861–1865).

The Civil War was fought between the Union of northern states and the Confederacy of southern states. The conflict was also known as the War Between the States. Fighting began on April 12, 1861, when Confederate artillery fired on Fort Sumter in the harbor at Charleston, South Carolina. Many people thought the war would be over quickly, but during the summer, neither side could claim a decisive

victory.

People feared the war might end with the United States broken into two nations, one in the south and one in the north.

Mark R. Watkinson preached the gospel at a congregation in the southern city of Richmond, Virginia. When war broke out, he moved north. A congregation at Ridleyville, Pennsylvania (now Prospect Park, Pennsylvania), invited him to be their minister. He'd served there years earlier as a young man before leaving to gain a better education and more experience. Upon his return as a full-time preacher, he earned a salary of 260 dollars a year.

Money was worth more then. A working person could live on 100 dollars a year. Daily expenses were less than a dollar. People carried coins to pay for their purchases. The **mint** stamped out a variety of small coins as well as valuable 10- and 20-dollar gold pieces.

Mark Watkinson knew that none of the coins carried any mention of God. He was concerned that the Civil War might end and the United States cease to exist. Future generations that looked at United States coins would see no reference to God. Watkinson wanted coins to show that America believed in God.

On November 13, 1861, Watkinson wrote to Salmon P. Chase, Secretary of the Treasury. Watkinson's letter read, "One fact touching our currency has hitherto been seriously overlooked. I mean the recognition

of the Almighty God in some form on our coins. . . . You are probably a Christian. What if our Republic were shattered beyond **reconstruction**. Would not the antiquaries [historians] of succeeding centuries rightly reason from our past that we were a **heathen** nation?"

Secretary Chase agreed with Watkinson. Within a week, he instructed James Pollock, Director of the Mint at Philadelphia, to prepare a motto. Chase wrote: "No nation can be strong except in the strength of God, nor safe except in His defense. The trust of our people in God should be declared on our national coins."

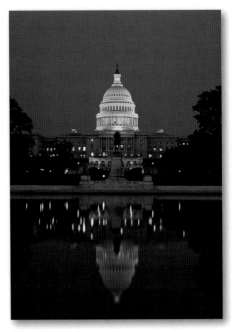

Small coins do not have room for long sayings. Director Pollock reread the letter from Secretary Chase. The phrase "The trust of our people in God" caught his attention. He shortened it to "In God We Trust."

Putting words on coins without approval of the **legislature** was forbidden by a law passed by Congress in 1837. Secretary Chase submitted a request for the change to Congress and won its approval in 1864. "In God We Trust" appeared for the first time on the front of an 1864 two-cent bronze coin. After that it was placed

on other coins, and in 1909, on the Lincoln penny. "In God We Trust" has appeared more than 300 billion times on the Lincoln cent alone.

Abraham Lincoln (1809-1865), president during the Civil War, said, "But for (the Bible) we could not know right from wrong. All things most desirable for man's welfare … are to be found portrayed in it."

Mark R. Watkinson was born in 1824. In October, 1850, He began working at the First Particular Baptist Church in Ridleyville. The church was made of stone, about 30 by 40 feet. He met and married Sarah I. Griffith while at the church. Later, he and his wife moved to Richmond, Virginia. When he returned to Ridleyville at the start of the Civil War, the preacher he replaced became postmaster for the town. Watkinson died in 1878, and his efforts for "In God We Trust" were largely forgotten. Research was done in the 1950s when the phrase was put on paper money, and his role was rediscovered. A plaque was placed at the site of Watkinson's Ridleyville church. Ridleyville is now Prospect Park, Pennsylvania.

Postage stamp money.

During the Civil War, coins became so scarce that people began using postage stamps for money. Two- and three-cent coins were minted to overcome the shortage. In the story "Gift of the Magi" by O. Henry (William Sydney Porter, 1862-1910), the heroine is described as having $1.87 with 60 cents of that in pennies. This would not be possible with the coins in use today, but at the time the story was written in 1906, two- and three-cent coins were still in circulation.

Trial mottoes. Secretary Chase and Mint Director Pollock wrote back and forth several times before they settled on "In God We Trust" to put on coins. Some of the other ideas included, "God, Law, Liberty," "Our Country And Our God," and "God, Our Trust."

The Source of In God We Trust

The quotation "In God is our trust" from Secretary Chase's letter was a patriotic expression from a well-known song. The song had been written 50 years earlier during the dark days of the War of 1812. The conflict between the United States and **Great Britain** began in June 1812 and lasted until January 1815.

Great Britain had been at war with the armies of Napoleon Bonaparte, the emperor of France. England needed sailors to staff its ships and fight its battles. The British illegally stopped American ships on the open seas. They searched American ships for war supplies, seized American

sailors, and made them fight for the British. The United States objected. President James Madison declared war.

At first, the United States won some battles. But in 1814, Napoleon was defeated — temporarily as it turned out — and England launched a fierce attack on the United States. In August 1814, British troops marched into Washington, D.C. The **Redcoats** set fire to the Capitol, the President's Mansion, and other public buildings. President James Madison and government officials fled the city.

After their victory in Washington, the British soldiers marched north to attack the important city of Baltimore, Maryland.

British ships carried supplies for the soldiers. Old and crumbling Fort McHenry stood between Baltimore and the 16 powerful British warships. British Admiral Alexander Cochrane believed his forces would quickly destroy the fort. If the American flag came down in surrender, British ships could safely sail to Baltimore.

Before the battle began, a young American lawyer named Francis Scott Key rowed out to the British ship under the white flag of truce. He came on a dangerous mission to rescue an American doctor who had been taken prisoner. Key carried letters from President Madison and from British soldiers. The letters proved that Dr. William Beanes was a civilian and had not been fighting the British. Wounded British soldiers praised the good doctor for treating them with the same care that he had given to American soldiers.

Admiral Cochrane agreed to release Francis Scott Key and Dr. Beanes, but not until after the battle was over.

The battle began at 7:00 a.m. on the morning of September 13. The fort should have been pounded into surrender within a few hours. Yet, 12 hours later as darkness fell, the American flag still flew over the fort. Throughout the intense fighting that night, Francis Scott Key stood at the railing of the British ship. He strained his eyes to glimpse the flag.

At daybreak a wonderful sight greeted the American. The defenders of Old Fort McHenry had managed to withstand 25 hours of shelling from the British ships. The **stars and stripes** still waved above the fort. The British sea forces stalled. The land attack was repelled. The British withdrew. Baltimore was saved.

Although Admiral Cochrane had lost the battle, he kept his word. He released Francis Scott Key and Dr. Beanes.

Once Francis Scott Key reached Baltimore he checked into the Indian Queen Hotel. He had written notes on the back of an envelope earlier that morning while aboard the British vessel. Now he referred to his notes as he composed a poem about the battle. He called his poem the "Defense of Fort M'Henry."

Late in the evening of the first day of the battle, he had seen the American flag over Fort McHenry. He described the time as "by twilight's last gleaming."

Rain, fog, and the smoke of gunpowder swirled

around the fort during the night. He could catch glimpses of the flag because the British shot off Congreve rockets. The fiery rockets, like gigantic bottle rockets, were intended to set ablaze the wooden structures inside the fort. Key could see the progress of the battle after dark because of the "rockets' red glare."

From two miles away, mighty cannons aboard British ships fired 13-inch cast iron exploding shells. The British shot 1,500 of the shells packed with 200 pounds of gunpowder at Fort McHenry. Lighted fuses were supposed to ignite the gunpowder as the shells hit their targets. However, because of pouring rain, some of the shells failed to explode. Others went off too soon.

Key wrote, "bombs bursting in the air gave proof through the night that the flag was still there." The next morning in "dawn's early light" at the end of the "perilous fight" the "star-spangled banner" still waved. He used the repeating refrain of "o'er the land of the free and the home of the brave."

Now he came to the end of his poem. On the last line of the last verse he penned the words: "Then conquer we must, for our cause it is just — and this be our motto — 'In God is our trust!'"

He set the poem to music from a song written

by John Stafford Smith, an English historian of music and a songwriter. Within a week, Key's composition was printed in the Baltimore *Patriot* newspaper. The song became popular and its title was changed to "The Star–Spangled Banner."

The phrase "In God is our trust!" from the song was the source of "In God We Trust" used first on American coins and later on paper money.

Dolly Madison to the Rescue. When the British attacked Washington, D.C., First Lady Dolly Madison, President Madison's wife, refused to leave the presidential mansion until important national treasures were packed and removed. She took with her the famous Gilbert Stuart portrait of George Washington and a copy of the Declaration of Independence. Although the British set the building afire, a steady rain doused the flames before they completely destroyed the building. When Dolly returned, she supervised the repair of the building. She had the soot marks covered by painting the building white.

Unlike the other buildings that were made of red brick, the president's mansion was made of white limestone. With the new paint, the building was a dazzling white, so the president's residence became known as the White House.

Fort McHenry. The fort was named for James McHenry, one of the patriots of the American Revolution (1775-1783). He had been one of the signers of the

constitution and also served as Secretary of War for John Adams, the second president of the United States.

Francis Scott Key, lawyer. After the War of 1812, Francis Scott Key (1779-1843) practiced law in Baltimore and Washington, D.C. He continued to write poetry. In 1834, he published a book titled *The Power of Literature and Its Connection with Religion.*

Stars and Stripes. The Stars and Stripes that flew over Fort McHenry had 15 stars and 15 stripes, representing the 15 states at that time. At first, a new star and a new stripe had been added for each new state that came into the Union. In 1818, it was decided to reduce the number of stripes to 13 and only add a star for each new state. Alaska added the last star to the flag in 1960 when it joined the Union, bringing the total to 50 stars.

Star-Spangled Banner. Mrs. Mary Pickersgill of Baltimore made the flag that flew at Fort McHenry. With the help of her daughter, she sewed it together in about a month at a cost of $405.90. It was a large flag, about 30 by 42 feet, with stars two feet across. The flag is displayed at the National Museum of American History in Washington, D.C. Souvenir hunters cut off the missing pieces before the National Museum took charge of it.

The National Anthem. Although the "Star-Spangled Banner" was played by military bands and sung at patriotic events, more than 100 years passed before it became the national anthem. Following the stock market crash of 1929, the country was plunged into the Great Depression. Business came to a standstill and people could not find work. American citizens needed a boost to their confidence. The "Star-Spangled Banner" told how Fort McHenry survived despite difficult times. On March 3, 1931, Congress made Key's song the national anthem.

A Nation Founded on Trust in God

Religious

people who trusted God to guide their lives settled America.
From the beginning, American statesmen sought God's
guidance as they governed the new nation.

Lawmakers such as George Washington, Thomas
Jefferson, and John Adams knew that dictators tried to place
themselves above any earthly power. These evil rulers tried
to control what people said, such as talking about their faith.
Dictators tried to limit what a person could read, including the
Bible. The existence of a higher authority — God — reminds

people that nobody is powerful enough to take away the freedom of others. Government does not have the final rule.

One of the first symbols of America was the Great Seal of the United States. Both sides of this circular design can be seen on the back of a one-dollar bill.

The front of the seal has an eagle that tells the story of the United States in symbols. The eagle grasps a bundle of arrows in the **talons** of one foot. The arrows stand for military strength. With its other talons, it holds an olive branch, a symbol of peace. The eagle clutches in its beak a ribbon with "e pluribus unum" written on it. The words are

Latin and mean "from many, one." The United States became one nation from 13 **colonies**.

The number 13 represents the 13 original colonies. It occurs many times on the seal. Above the eagle's head is a cloud filled with 13 stars. The eagle has a shield across its chest with 13 stripes. The claw holds 13 arrows, and the olive branch has 13 leaves with 13 olives.

On the other side of the Great Seal, the main picture is a pyramid such as those found in Egypt. A pyramid is a strong building, a symbol of the strength of the United States. On the bottom layer of the stone pyramid is the date 1776, in Roman numerals: MDCCLXXVI. American patriots met in

Philadelphia in July 1776. They took the bold and dangerous action of declaring independence from England.

A scroll below the pyramid bears the Latin words, "novus ordo seclorum," which means "new order of the ages."

The year 1776 became the first year that a major country was governed by the vote of its citizens. The top of the pyramid is incomplete, showing that the work of **democracy** is never finished.

Above the pyramid is a triangle in a burst of light called glory. Inside the triangle is one large eye — the all-seeing eye of God. Prominently displayed above the eye are the words "annuit coeptis," which mean "God favored our undertaking."

Congress adopted the design of the Great Seal in June 1782. The seal with the all-seeing eye of God and the words that mean "God favored our undertaking" was first used on coins in 1795.

In the early days of the United States, Latin was the language of scholars. Educated people who spoke French, German, Italian, or English also knew Latin. They could communicate with one another in Latin. When the founders of the United States put "annuit coeptis" on the Great Seal, they knew that most educated people would understand its meaning.

Later, the general population gained an education but could only read and write English. Few people understood the meaning of the Latin words. By the 1860s, it became important to express the nation's belief in God in English words. "In God We Trust" fulfilled this very evident need.

Annuit coeptis. Although "God favored our undertaking" is the best-known way to translate "annuit coeptis," the words can also mean "God smiled on our undertaking."

Mary Washington, George Washington's mother, said, "Remember that God is our only sure trust."

Samuel Adams (1722-1803) of Massachusetts said at the signing of the Declaration of Independence, "We have this day restored the Sovereign to who alone men ought to be obedient. He reigns in heaven and from the rising to the setting sun may His kingdom come."

William Penn (1644-1718), an English Quaker who oversaw establishing Pennsylvania, said, "Men must be governed by God, or they will be ruled by tyrants."

Women on Money. Early American coins had a female figure to represent liberty on them. Martha Washington is the only woman whose portrait has appeared on United States paper money. Her portrait appeared on the front of a one dollar-bill in 1886.

In God We Trust Today

Although

Congress agreed that "In God We Trust" could be on coins, they did not require its use. Some coins, such as the Liberty Head nickel **minted** between 1883 and 1913, and the Buffalo nickel minted between 1913 and 1938, did not have the motto. In 1907, the

words were intentionally dropped from the newly minted 10- and 20-dollar gold pieces. The public outcry caused Congress to restore the motto.

During three years in the 1950s, Congress passed several important resolutions that President Eisenhower signed into law. In 1954, the words "under God" were added to the Pledge of Allegiance, and the phrase "so help me God" was added to the oath of office for federal judges. In 1955, "In God We Trust" was put on American money. The law said, "The inscription shall appear on all United States currency and coins." The next year, 1956, "In God We Trust" became the official national motto of the United States. It was inscribed on national monuments, on the walls of courthouses, and in the halls of government buildings.

Because "In God We Trust" is the national motto, banners and posters with the words can be put in public buildings including schools. In 1977, the United States Supreme Court upheld use of the motto.

The United States is the only country in the world that has a religious motto.

The words are a reminder that God is central to the nation's success. Every time the United States has been in difficult times, people have turned to God. As the new nation struggled into existence in the late 1700s, the Great Seal of the

United States carried Latin words meaning "God favored our undertaking." During the War of 1812, Francis Scott Key's words "And this be our motto — In God is our trust" filled people with patriotism and resolve.

The Civil War of the 1860s nearly tore the nation apart, but coins for the first time carried the phrase "In God We Trust." In the 1950s, the troublesome times of the Cold War and the threat of global war drew people closer to God. Soviet communism collapsed in the 1980s.

Today, many schools in Russia have welcomed missionaries into the classrooms to talk about Christianity and give Bibles to the students. However, in the United States that is not the case. Prayer, display of religious scenes, and quotations from the Bible have been taken out of public places.

The terrorist attack on September 11, 2001, marked a new era in American history. The war on terrorism reminded people that God needed to be invited back into the daily life of the nation.

Christian believers agree with the Bible verse that says, "If my people, which are called by my name, shall humble themselves, and pray, and seek my face, and turn from their wicked ways; then will I hear from heaven, and will forgive their sin, and will heal their land" (2 Chronicles 7:14).

Patrick Henry (1736-1799), patriot and first governor of the state of Virginia is best known for the statement, "Give me liberty or give me death." He also said, "God presides over the destinies of nations."

On the Jefferson Memorial in

Washington, D.C., are words by Thomas Jefferson (1743-1826): "God who gave us life gave us liberty. Can the liberties of a nation be secure when we have removed a conviction that these liberties are the gift of God?"

Presidents on paper money include George Washington ($1), Thomas Jefferson ($2), Abraham Lincoln ($5), Andrew Jackson ($20), Ulysses Grant ($50). Alexander Hamilton, the first Secretary of the Treasury, is on the ten-dollar bill. Benjamin Franklin, one of the signers of the Declaration of Independence, is on the 100-dollar bill.

Weighing Money. All bills, regardless of their value, weigh about one gram each, or about 454 bills to the pound. If an 80-pound child were worth his or her weight in one-dollar bills, he or she would be worth about 36,320 dollars.

Questions

<u>A B</u> Abut two-thirds of all the United States currency is
(A. inside the United States   B. in other countries).

<u>A B</u> Until the 1950s, the phrase "In God We Trust" was
only on (A. coins   B. paper money).

<u>A B C D</u> The person who worked to put "In God We
Trust" on paper money was (A. lawyer Francis Scott
Key   B. minister Mark R. Watkinson
C. furniture store owner Matthew Rothert
D. First Lady Dolly Madison).

The phrase "In God We Trust" first appeared on coins
during what war? _____

<u>A B C D</u> During the 1860s, most people paid for their
purchases with (A. charge cards   B. checks
C. coins   D. paper money).

<u>T F</u> Mark Watkinson was concerned that historians
of the future might think the United States was a
heathen nation.

<u>A B</u> One of the reasons for the War of 1812 was because
the British (A. refused to pay American tea taxes
B. seized American sailors).

<u>A B C D</u> Francis Scott Key wrote the "Star-Spangled
Banner" while observing the bombardment of (A. Fort
McHenry   B. Gettysburg   C. Statue of Liberty
D. Washington, D.C).

A B C D All of the following phrases are written in
Latin on the Great Seal of the United States except (A.
"from many, one"   B. "God favored our undertaking"
C. "In God We Trust"   D. "new order of the ages").

A B C D "In God We Trust" became the national motto
during the presidential term of (A. Abraham Lincoln
B. Dwight Eisenhower   C. George Washington
D. James Madison).

T F The United States is the only country in the world with a
religious motto.

Answers to Questions

B in other countries

A coins

C furniture salesman Matthew Rothert

Civil War

C coins

T

B seized American sailors

A Fort McHenry

C In God We Trust

B Dwight Eisenhower

T

Activities

Examine each of the coins in use in the United States today. What phrases are written on the coins? Do all coins have the words "United States of America"? Do all of them have the motto "In God We Trust"? Is the motto on the obverse or reverse? Research how coins are made and summarize the process. What metals are used in the coins?

Which coins of the United States have milling (fine grooves) along their edges? Which of them are smooth along their edges? With a friend, put several coins of each denomination (penny, nickel, dime, quarter, half-dollar) in a sock. When a friend names a coin, use the sense of touch to find the right coin and pull it out.

Examine the back of a one-dollar bill. How many times can you find the word "one" or the numeral "1"? How many layers of rock make the pyramid? Locate the words "annuit coeptis," "novus ordo seclorum," the Roman numerals MDCCLXXVI, "e plurus unum," the Great Seal of the United States, and "In God We Trust." Read and report about steps that the government takes to make it difficult to counterfeit money.

Ask several people, "Do you think it would be all right to post the national motto in public school classrooms?" Ask, "What is the national motto of the United States?" How many know that the motto is "In God We Trust"? How does their answer about posting the motto change when you reveal that the national motto is "In God We Trust"?

Draw a poster with the words "In God We Trust" on it. Decorate the poster with some of the other symbols of the nation such as the American bald eagle, the Statue of Liberty, and the American flag.

Write a poem that expresses your faith and trust in God.

Write a short biography about one of the following individuals:

>   John Adams
>   Winston Churchill
>   Dwight D. Eisenhower
>   Abraham Lincoln
>   Dolly Madison
>   George Washington

Glossary

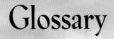

In 1607, European settlers established the first of 13 colonies in Jamestown, Virginia. The 13 colonies remained under British rule until they declared independence in 1776.

A **communist** government has a dictator or small group of leaders who hold power and control the economy. Private property is outlawed, and rights of individuals are restricted. Many countries that tried communism in the early 1900s abandoned the idea by the end of the 1900s.

A **counterfeit** coin or bill is an illegal copy.

Congress is the national legislative body of the United States, consisting of the Senate and the House of Representatives. Congress makes laws that govern the nation.

A **democracy** is a government in which the people make decisions about how the country is run. Democracies are noted for giving citizens individual liberties including freedom of speech and worship.

The **economy** of a country is how its system for producing goods and services is managed. The people of a country with a strong economy can feed, clothe, and house themselves despite hard times such as war or natural disasters.

The **first lady** is the president's wife. She is hostess for visitors to the White House and can take on other duties of her own choosing.

England, Scotland, and Wales make up the country of Great Britain. Often, people say "England" or "the British" to refer to Great Britain.

A heathen is a person or nation that does not recognize the God of the Bible.

The legislature of a nation is the group of people who have been elected to make laws.

Coins are minted by stamping a design onto a blank metal disk.

The obverse of a coin is the front or "heads."

Reconstruction was the rebuilding of the South after the Civil War. Reconstruction lasted from 1865 to 1877. During that time, the federal government was put in charge of the southern states.

Soldiers of Great Britain during the Revolutionary War and the War of 1812 were called Redcoats because their uniforms included red coats.

The reverse of a coin is the back or "tails."

Stars and stripes is the name given to the flag of the United States. The flag is also known as Old Glory and the Star-Spangled Banner.

Talons are the claws of birds of prey such as eagles or hawks.

The different values of money in circulation are the denominations. United States paper money comes in denominations of $1, $2, $5, $10, $20, $50, and $100.